D1593288

THE
SELF-
LOVE
JOURNAL

KELSEY LAYNE

A TarcherPerigee Book

I am kind to myself

ESPECIALLY ON BAD DAYS

FALL IN LOVE WITH YOU

✦ ✦

BECAUSE YOU ARE AMAZING!

Self-love is everything. It allows us to connect with
our inner magic, and has the power to make us feel
inner peace and pure joy. But it can be hard to
find time to show ourselves love when the stresses
of day-to-day life take over.

This journal will prompt you to give your mind, body,
and soul the love that you deserve and will help
you to fall in love with you.

Kelsey x

WEEK BEGINNING _____

I LOVE MYSELF BECAUSE:

1. _____

2. _____

3. _____

EMPOWERING AFFIRMATION:

THIS WEEK FOR SELF-CARE I WILL:

_____

_____

_____

_____

THIS WEEK I CHALLENGE MYSELF TO:

_____

_____

_____

THE HOBBY I WILL MAKE TIME FOR IS:

_____

_____

I WILL NOURISH MY BODY
WITH THE FOLLOWING HEALTHY MEALS:

_____   FREE FLOW / REFLECTION   _____

✴ SACRED SPACE ✴

REFLECT, SET INTENTIONS, OR FREE-FLOW JOURNAL.

I make* time for the things that bring me **true joy**

WEEK BEGINNING _____

I LOVE MYSELF BECAUSE:

1. _____

2. _____

3. _____

EMPOWERING AFFIRMATION:

THIS WEEK FOR SELF-CARE I WILL:

THIS WEEK I CHALLENGE MYSELF TO:

THE HOBBY I WILL MAKE TIME FOR IS:

_____

_____

**I WILL NOURISH MY BODY
WITH THE FOLLOWING HEALTHY MEALS:**

_____ **FREE FLOW / REFLECTION** _____

WEEK BEGINNING _____

I LOVE MYSELF BECAUSE:

1. _____

2. _____

3. _____

EMPOWERING AFFIRMATION:

THIS WEEK FOR SELF-CARE I WILL:

_____

_____

_____

_____

THIS WEEK I CHALLENGE MYSELF TO:

_____

_____

_____

THE HOBBY I WILL MAKE TIME FOR IS:

_____

_____

**I WILL NOURISH MY BODY
WITH THE FOLLOWING HEALTHY MEALS:**

_____ **FREE FLOW / REFLECTION** _____

✳ SACRED SPACE ✳

REFLECT, SET INTENTIONS, OR FREE-FLOW JOURNAL.

I give myself the time I need

TO REFLECT AND BE STILL

WEEK BEGINNING _____

I LOVE MYSELF BECAUSE:

1. _____

2. _____

3. _____

EMPOWERING AFFIRMATION:

THIS WEEK FOR SELF-CARE I WILL:

_____

_____

_____

THIS WEEK I CHALLENGE MYSELF TO:

_____

_____

_____

THE HOBBY I WILL MAKE TIME FOR IS:

_____

_____

I WILL NOURISH MY BODY
WITH THE FOLLOWING HEALTHY MEALS:

_____ FREE FLOW / REFLECTION _____

WEEK BEGINNING _____

I LOVE MYSELF BECAUSE:

1. _____

2. _____

3. _____

EMPOWERING AFFIRMATION:

THIS WEEK FOR SELF-CARE I WILL:

_____

_____

_____

_____

THIS WEEK I CHALLENGE MYSELF TO:

_____

_____

_____

THE HOBBY I WILL MAKE TIME FOR IS:

_____

_____

I WILL NOURISH MY BODY
WITH THE FOLLOWING HEALTHY MEALS:

_____   FREE FLOW / REFLECTION   _____

✳ SACRED SPACE ✳

REFLECT, SET INTENTIONS, OR FREE-FLOW JOURNAL.

I

confidently

follow

my

own

path

WEEK BEGINNING _____

I LOVE MYSELF BECAUSE:

1. _____

2. _____

3. _____

EMPOWERING AFFIRMATION:

```
┌──────────────────────────────────────────┐
│                                            │
│                                            │
│                                            │
│                                            │
└──────────────────────────────────────────┘
```

THIS WEEK FOR SELF-CARE I WILL:

_____

_____

_____

_____

THIS WEEK I CHALLENGE MYSELF TO:

_____

_____

_____

THE HOBBY I WILL MAKE TIME FOR IS:

_____

_____

**I WILL NOURISH MY BODY
WITH THE FOLLOWING HEALTHY MEALS:**

_____   **FREE FLOW / REFLECTION**   _____

WEEK BEGINNING _____

I LOVE MYSELF BECAUSE:

1. _____

2. _____

3. _____

EMPOWERING AFFIRMATION:

THIS WEEK FOR SELF-CARE I WILL:

_____

_____

_____

_____

THIS WEEK I CHALLENGE MYSELF TO:

_____

_____

_____

THE HOBBY I WILL MAKE TIME FOR IS:

_____

_____

I WILL NOURISH MY BODY
WITH THE FOLLOWING HEALTHY MEALS:

_____   **FREE FLOW / REFLECTION**   _____

✳ SACRED SPACE ✳

REFLECT, SET INTENTIONS, OR FREE-FLOW JOURNAL.

Self-Care

♥ EQUALS ♥

Self-Love

WEEK BEGINNING _____

I LOVE MYSELF BECAUSE:

1. _____

2. _____

3. _____

EMPOWERING AFFIRMATION:

THIS WEEK FOR SELF-CARE I WILL:

_____

_____

_____

_____

THIS WEEK I CHALLENGE MYSELF TO:

_____

_____

_____

THE HOBBY I WILL MAKE TIME FOR IS:

_____

_____

**I WILL NOURISH MY BODY
WITH THE FOLLOWING HEALTHY MEALS:**

_____ **FREE FLOW / REFLECTION** _____

WEEK BEGINNING _____

I LOVE MYSELF BECAUSE:

1. _____

2. _____

3. _____

EMPOWERING AFFIRMATION:

THIS WEEK FOR SELF-CARE I WILL:

_____

_____

_____

_____

THIS WEEK I CHALLENGE MYSELF TO:

_____

_____

_____

THE HOBBY I WILL MAKE TIME FOR IS:

I WILL NOURISH MY BODY
WITH THE FOLLOWING HEALTHY MEALS:

FREE FLOW / REFLECTION

✳ SACRED SPACE ✳

REFLECT, SET INTENTIONS, OR FREE-FLOW JOURNAL.

I CHOOSE
HAPPINESS

WEEK BEGINNING _____

I LOVE MYSELF BECAUSE:

1. _____

2. _____

3. _____

EMPOWERING AFFIRMATION:

THIS WEEK FOR SELF-CARE I WILL:

_____

_____

_____

_____

THIS WEEK I CHALLENGE MYSELF TO:

_____

_____

_____

THE HOBBY I WILL MAKE TIME FOR IS:

_____

_____

I WILL NOURISH MY BODY
WITH THE FOLLOWING HEALTHY MEALS:

_____ FREE FLOW / REFLECTION _____

WEEK BEGINNING _____

I LOVE MYSELF BECAUSE:

1. _____

2. _____

3. _____

EMPOWERING AFFIRMATION:

THIS WEEK FOR SELF-CARE I WILL:

_____

_____

_____

_____

THIS WEEK I CHALLENGE MYSELF TO:

_____

_____

_____

THE HOBBY I WILL MAKE TIME FOR IS:

_____

_____

I WILL NOURISH MY BODY
WITH THE FOLLOWING HEALTHY MEALS:

_____ **FREE FLOW / REFLECTION** _____

✳ SACRED SPACE ✳

REFLECT, SET INTENTIONS, OR FREE-FLOW JOURNAL.

♥ I CAN ♥
HEAL ANY
WOUND
THAT
I CARRY

WEEK BEGINNING _____

I LOVE MYSELF BECAUSE:

1.
_____

2.
_____

3.
_____

EMPOWERING AFFIRMATION:

THIS WEEK FOR SELF-CARE I WILL:

_____

_____

_____

_____

THIS WEEK I CHALLENGE MYSELF TO:

_____

_____

_____

THE HOBBY I WILL MAKE TIME FOR IS:

_____

_____

I WILL NOURISH MY BODY
WITH THE FOLLOWING HEALTHY MEALS:

_____ FREE FLOW / REFLECTION _____

WEEK BEGINNING _____

I LOVE MYSELF BECAUSE:

1. _____

2. _____

3. _____

EMPOWERING AFFIRMATION:

THIS WEEK FOR SELF-CARE I WILL:

_____

_____

_____

_____

THIS WEEK I CHALLENGE MYSELF TO:

_____

_____

_____

THE HOBBY I WILL MAKE TIME FOR IS:

_____

_____

I WILL NOURISH MY BODY
WITH THE FOLLOWING HEALTHY MEALS:

FREE FLOW / REFLECTION

✳ SACRED SPACE ✳

REFLECT, SET INTENTIONS, OR FREE-FLOW JOURNAL.

i AM
magical

WEEK BEGINNING _____

I LOVE MYSELF BECAUSE:

1. _____

2. _____

3. _____

EMPOWERING AFFIRMATION:

THIS WEEK FOR SELF-CARE I WILL:

_____

_____

_____

_____

THIS WEEK I CHALLENGE MYSELF TO:

_____

_____

_____

THE HOBBY I WILL MAKE TIME FOR IS:

_____

_____

I WILL NOURISH MY BODY
WITH THE FOLLOWING HEALTHY MEALS:

_____   **FREE FLOW / REFLECTION**   _____

WEEK BEGINNING _____

I LOVE MYSELF BECAUSE:

1. _____

2. _____

3. _____

EMPOWERING AFFIRMATION:

┌───┐
│   │
│   │
│   │
│   │
└───┘

THIS WEEK FOR SELF-CARE I WILL:

_____

_____

_____

_____

THIS WEEK I CHALLENGE MYSELF TO:

_____

_____

_____

THE HOBBY I WILL MAKE TIME FOR IS:

_____

_____

I WILL NOURISH MY BODY
WITH THE FOLLOWING HEALTHY MEALS:

_____ FREE FLOW / REFLECTION _____

✳ SACRED SPACE ✳

REFLECT, SET INTENTIONS, OR FREE-FLOW JOURNAL.

WEEK BEGINNING _____

I LOVE MYSELF BECAUSE:

1. _____

2. _____

3. _____

EMPOWERING AFFIRMATION:

_____

THIS WEEK FOR SELF-CARE I WILL:

_____

_____

_____

_____

THIS WEEK I CHALLENGE MYSELF TO:

_____

_____

_____

THE HOBBY I WILL MAKE TIME FOR IS:

_____

_____

**I WILL NOURISH MY BODY
WITH THE FOLLOWING HEALTHY MEALS:**

_____ **FREE FLOW / REFLECTION** _____

WEEK BEGINNING _____

I LOVE MYSELF BECAUSE:

1.

2.

3.

EMPOWERING AFFIRMATION:

THIS WEEK FOR SELF-CARE I WILL:

THIS WEEK I CHALLENGE MYSELF TO:

THE HOBBY I WILL MAKE TIME FOR IS:

_____

_____

I WILL NOURISH MY BODY
WITH THE FOLLOWING HEALTHY MEALS:

_____   **FREE FLOW / REFLECTION**   _____

✷ SACRED SPACE ✷

REFLECT, SET INTENTIONS, OR FREE-FLOW JOURNAL.

I flow calmly

THROUGH ANY CHALLENGE THAT MAY ARISE

WEEK BEGINNING _____

I LOVE MYSELF BECAUSE:

1. _____

2. _____

3. _____

EMPOWERING AFFIRMATION:

THIS WEEK FOR SELF-CARE I WILL:

_____

_____

_____

_____

THIS WEEK I CHALLENGE MYSELF TO:

_____

_____

_____

THE HOBBY I WILL MAKE TIME FOR IS:

_____

_____

**I WILL NOURISH MY BODY
WITH THE FOLLOWING HEALTHY MEALS:**

_____   **FREE FLOW / REFLECTION**   _____

WEEK BEGINNING _____

I LOVE MYSELF BECAUSE:

1. _____

2. _____

3. _____

EMPOWERING AFFIRMATION:

THIS WEEK FOR SELF-CARE I WILL:

_____

_____

_____

_____

THIS WEEK I CHALLENGE MYSELF TO:

_____

_____

_____

THE HOBBY I WILL MAKE TIME FOR IS:

_____

_____

**I WILL NOURISH MY BODY
WITH THE FOLLOWING HEALTHY MEALS:**

_____   **FREE FLOW / REFLECTION**   _____

✳ SACRED SPACE ✳

REFLECT, SET INTENTIONS, OR FREE-FLOW JOURNAL.

I am
patient
with
myself
as I grow
and
heal

WEEK BEGINNING _____

I LOVE MYSELF BECAUSE:

1. _____

2. _____

3. _____

EMPOWERING AFFIRMATION:

THIS WEEK FOR SELF-CARE I WILL:

_____

_____

_____

_____

THIS WEEK I CHALLENGE MYSELF TO:

_____

_____

_____

THE HOBBY I WILL MAKE TIME FOR IS:

_____

_____

**I WILL NOURISH MY BODY
WITH THE FOLLOWING HEALTHY MEALS:**

_____   **FREE FLOW / REFLECTION**   _____

WEEK BEGINNING _____

I LOVE MYSELF BECAUSE:

1. _____

2. _____

3. _____

EMPOWERING AFFIRMATION:

_____

THIS WEEK FOR SELF-CARE I WILL:

_____

_____

_____

_____

THIS WEEK I CHALLENGE MYSELF TO:

_____

_____

_____

THE HOBBY I WILL MAKE TIME FOR IS:

_____

_____

**I WILL NOURISH MY BODY
WITH THE FOLLOWING HEALTHY MEALS:**

_____ **FREE FLOW / REFLECTION** _____

✴ SACRED SPACE ✴

REFLECT, SET INTENTIONS, OR FREE-FLOW JOURNAL.

♥ I AM ♥
BEAUTIFUL

WEEK BEGINNING _____

I LOVE MYSELF BECAUSE:

1. _____

2. _____

3. _____

EMPOWERING AFFIRMATION:

THIS WEEK FOR SELF-CARE I WILL:

_____

_____

_____

_____

THIS WEEK I CHALLENGE MYSELF TO:

_____

_____

_____

THE HOBBY I WILL MAKE TIME FOR IS:

_____

_____

I WILL NOURISH MY BODY
WITH THE FOLLOWING HEALTHY MEALS:

_____ **FREE FLOW / REFLECTION** _____

WEEK BEGINNING _____

I LOVE MYSELF BECAUSE:

1. _____

2. _____

3. _____

EMPOWERING AFFIRMATION:

THIS WEEK FOR SELF-CARE I WILL:

_____

_____

_____

_____

THIS WEEK I CHALLENGE MYSELF TO:

_____

_____

_____

THE HOBBY I WILL MAKE TIME FOR IS:

_____

_____

I WILL NOURISH MY BODY
WITH THE FOLLOWING HEALTHY MEALS:

_____   **FREE FLOW / REFLECTION**   _____

✳ SACRED SPACE ✳

REFLECT, SET INTENTIONS, OR FREE-FLOW JOURNAL.

I
LISTEN TO
MY
BODY

WEEK BEGINNING _____

I LOVE MYSELF BECAUSE:

1. _____

2. _____

3. _____

EMPOWERING AFFIRMATION:

THIS WEEK FOR SELF-CARE I WILL:

THIS WEEK I CHALLENGE MYSELF TO:

THE HOBBY I WILL MAKE TIME FOR IS:

_____

_____

I WILL NOURISH MY BODY
WITH THE FOLLOWING HEALTHY MEALS:

_____ FREE FLOW / REFLECTION _____

WEEK BEGINNING _____

I LOVE MYSELF BECAUSE:

1. _____

2. _____

3. _____

EMPOWERING AFFIRMATION:

THIS WEEK FOR SELF-CARE I WILL:

_____

_____

_____

_____

THIS WEEK I CHALLENGE MYSELF TO:

_____

_____

_____

THE HOBBY I WILL MAKE TIME FOR IS:

_____

_____

I WILL NOURISH MY BODY
WITH THE FOLLOWING HEALTHY MEALS:

_____   FREE FLOW / REFLECTION   _____

✳ SACRED SPACE ✳

REFLECT, SET INTENTIONS, OR FREE-FLOW JOURNAL.

I MAKE TIME FOR HEALING RITUALS

WEEK BEGINNING _____

I LOVE MYSELF BECAUSE:

1. _____

2. _____

3. _____

EMPOWERING AFFIRMATION:

THIS WEEK FOR SELF-CARE I WILL:

_____

_____

_____

THIS WEEK I CHALLENGE MYSELF TO:

_____

_____

THE HOBBY I WILL MAKE TIME FOR IS:

_____

_____

I WILL NOURISH MY BODY
WITH THE FOLLOWING HEALTHY MEALS:

_____   **FREE FLOW / REFLECTION**   _____

WEEK BEGINNING _____

I LOVE MYSELF BECAUSE:

1. _____

2. _____

3. _____

EMPOWERING AFFIRMATION:

THIS WEEK FOR SELF-CARE I WILL:

_____

_____

_____

_____

THIS WEEK I CHALLENGE MYSELF TO:

_____

_____

_____

THE HOBBY I WILL MAKE TIME FOR IS:

_____

_____

I WILL NOURISH MY BODY
WITH THE FOLLOWING HEALTHY MEALS:

_____ FREE FLOW / REFLECTION _____

✳ SACRED SPACE ✳

REFLECT, SET INTENTIONS, OR FREE-FLOW JOURNAL.

I CAN EASILY ACCESS ✳ MY ✳ GIFTS

WEEK BEGINNING _____

I LOVE MYSELF BECAUSE:

1. _____

2. _____

3. _____

EMPOWERING AFFIRMATION:

THIS WEEK FOR SELF-CARE I WILL:

_____

_____

_____

_____

THIS WEEK I CHALLENGE MYSELF TO:

_____

_____

_____

THE HOBBY I WILL MAKE TIME FOR IS:

_____

_____

**I WILL NOURISH MY BODY
WITH THE FOLLOWING HEALTHY MEALS:**

_____   **FREE FLOW / REFLECTION**   _____

WEEK BEGINNING _____

I LOVE MYSELF BECAUSE:

1. _____

2. _____

3. _____

EMPOWERING AFFIRMATION:

THIS WEEK FOR SELF-CARE I WILL:

_____

_____

_____

_____

THIS WEEK I CHALLENGE MYSELF TO:

_____

_____

_____

THE HOBBY I WILL MAKE TIME FOR IS:

_____

_____

I WILL NOURISH MY BODY
WITH THE FOLLOWING HEALTHY MEALS:

FREE FLOW / REFLECTION

✷ SACRED SPACE ✷

REFLECT, SET INTENTIONS, OR FREE-FLOW JOURNAL.

I surround

myself

with

LOVE

and

HAPPINESS

WEEK BEGINNING _____

I LOVE MYSELF BECAUSE:

1. _____

2. _____

3. _____

EMPOWERING AFFIRMATION:

┌──┐
│   │
│   │
│   │
│   │
└──┘

THIS WEEK FOR SELF-CARE I WILL:

_____

_____

_____

_____

THIS WEEK I CHALLENGE MYSELF TO:

_____

_____

_____

THE HOBBY I WILL MAKE TIME FOR IS:

_____

_____

I WILL NOURISH MY BODY
WITH THE FOLLOWING HEALTHY MEALS:

_____ FREE FLOW / REFLECTION _____

WEEK BEGINNING _____

I LOVE MYSELF BECAUSE:

1. _____

2. _____

3. _____

EMPOWERING AFFIRMATION:

THIS WEEK FOR SELF-CARE I WILL:

_____

_____

_____

_____

THIS WEEK I CHALLENGE MYSELF TO:

_____

_____

_____

THE HOBBY I WILL MAKE TIME FOR IS:

_____

_____

I WILL NOURISH MY BODY
WITH THE FOLLOWING HEALTHY MEALS:

FREE FLOW / REFLECTION

WEEK BEGINNING _____

I LOVE MYSELF BECAUSE:

1. _____

2. _____

3. _____

EMPOWERING AFFIRMATION:

THIS WEEK FOR SELF-CARE I WILL:

_____

_____

_____

_____

THIS WEEK I CHALLENGE MYSELF TO:

_____

_____

_____

THE HOBBY I WILL MAKE TIME FOR IS:

_____

_____

I WILL NOURISH MY BODY
WITH THE FOLLOWING HEALTHY MEALS:

_____ FREE FLOW / REFLECTION _____

WEEK BEGINNING _____

I LOVE MYSELF BECAUSE:

1.
_____

2.
_____

3.
_____

EMPOWERING AFFIRMATION:

THIS WEEK FOR SELF-CARE I WILL:

_____

_____

_____

_____

THIS WEEK I CHALLENGE MYSELF TO:

_____

_____

_____

THE HOBBY I WILL MAKE TIME FOR IS:

_____

_____

I WILL NOURISH MY BODY
WITH THE FOLLOWING HEALTHY MEALS:

_____   FREE FLOW / REFLECTION   _____

WEEK BEGINNING _____

I LOVE MYSELF BECAUSE:

1. _____

2. _____

3. _____

EMPOWERING AFFIRMATION:

THIS WEEK FOR SELF-CARE I WILL:

_____

_____

_____

_____

THIS WEEK I CHALLENGE MYSELF TO:

_____

_____

_____

THE HOBBY I WILL MAKE TIME FOR IS:

_____

_____

**I WILL NOURISH MY BODY
WITH THE FOLLOWING HEALTHY MEALS:**

_____   **FREE FLOW / REFLECTION**   _____

✳ SACRED SPACE ✳

REFLECT, SET INTENTIONS, OR FREE-FLOW JOURNAL.

I AM
in tune
with
✷ MY ✷
INNER
BEING

WEEK BEGINNING _____

I LOVE MYSELF BECAUSE:

1. _____

2. _____

3. _____

EMPOWERING AFFIRMATION:

_____

THIS WEEK FOR SELF-CARE I WILL:

_____

_____

_____

_____

THIS WEEK I CHALLENGE MYSELF TO:

_____

_____

_____

THE HOBBY I WILL MAKE TIME FOR IS:

_____

_____

I WILL NOURISH MY BODY
WITH THE FOLLOWING HEALTHY MEALS:

_____ FREE FLOW / REFLECTION _____

WEEK BEGINNING _____

I LOVE MYSELF BECAUSE:

1. _____

2. _____

3. _____

EMPOWERING AFFIRMATION:

THIS WEEK FOR SELF-CARE I WILL:

THIS WEEK I CHALLENGE MYSELF TO:

THE HOBBY I WILL MAKE TIME FOR IS:

_____

_____

**I WILL NOURISH MY BODY
WITH THE FOLLOWING HEALTHY MEALS:**

_____ **FREE FLOW / REFLECTION** _____

✳ SACRED SPACE ✳

REFLECT, SET INTENTIONS, OR FREE-FLOW JOURNAL.

I MAKE ☀TIME☀ TO GROUND MYSELF IN NATURE

WEEK BEGINNING _____

I LOVE MYSELF BECAUSE:

1. _____

2. _____

3. _____

EMPOWERING AFFIRMATION:

THIS WEEK FOR SELF-CARE I WILL:

_____

_____

_____

_____

THIS WEEK I CHALLENGE MYSELF TO:

_____

_____

_____

THE HOBBY I WILL MAKE TIME FOR IS:

_____

_____

I WILL NOURISH MY BODY
WITH THE FOLLOWING HEALTHY MEALS:

_____ FREE FLOW / REFLECTION _____

WEEK BEGINNING _____

I LOVE MYSELF BECAUSE:

1.
_____

2.
_____

3.
_____

EMPOWERING AFFIRMATION:

THIS WEEK FOR SELF-CARE I WILL:

_____

_____

_____

_____

THIS WEEK I CHALLENGE MYSELF TO:

_____

_____

_____

THE HOBBY I WILL MAKE TIME FOR IS:

_____

_____

**I WILL NOURISH MY BODY
WITH THE FOLLOWING HEALTHY MEALS:**

_____ **FREE FLOW / REFLECTION** _____

✳ SACRED SPACE ✳

REFLECT, SET INTENTIONS, OR FREE-FLOW JOURNAL.

I

love

all

that

I am

WEEK BEGINNING _____

I LOVE MYSELF BECAUSE:

1.
_____

2.
_____

3.
_____

EMPOWERING AFFIRMATION:

THIS WEEK FOR SELF-CARE I WILL:

_____

_____

_____

_____

THIS WEEK I CHALLENGE MYSELF TO:

_____

_____

_____

THE HOBBY I WILL MAKE TIME FOR IS:

_____

_____

**I WILL NOURISH MY BODY
WITH THE FOLLOWING HEALTHY MEALS:**

_____ **FREE FLOW / REFLECTION** _____

WEEK BEGINNING _____

I LOVE MYSELF BECAUSE:

1. _____

2. _____

3. _____

EMPOWERING AFFIRMATION:

THIS WEEK FOR SELF-CARE I WILL:

THIS WEEK I CHALLENGE MYSELF TO:

THE HOBBY I WILL MAKE TIME FOR IS:

_____

_____

I WILL NOURISH MY BODY
WITH THE FOLLOWING HEALTHY MEALS:

_____ FREE FLOW / REFLECTION _____

✳ SACRED SPACE ✳

REFLECT, SET INTENTIONS, OR FREE-FLOW JOURNAL.

I flow confidently with my own ENERGY

WEEK BEGINNING _____

I LOVE MYSELF BECAUSE:

1. _____

2. _____

3. _____

EMPOWERING AFFIRMATION:

THIS WEEK FOR SELF-CARE I WILL:

_____

_____

_____

_____

THIS WEEK I CHALLENGE MYSELF TO:

_____

_____

_____

THE HOBBY I WILL MAKE TIME FOR IS:

_____

_____

**I WILL NOURISH MY BODY
WITH THE FOLLOWING HEALTHY MEALS:**

_____ **FREE FLOW / REFLECTION** _____

WEEK BEGINNING _____

I LOVE MYSELF BECAUSE:

1. _____

2. _____

3. _____

EMPOWERING AFFIRMATION:

┌───┐
│   │
│   │
│   │
│   │
└───┘

THIS WEEK FOR SELF-CARE I WILL:

_____

_____

_____

_____

THIS WEEK I CHALLENGE MYSELF TO:

_____

_____

_____

THE HOBBY I WILL MAKE TIME FOR IS:

_____

_____

**I WILL NOURISH MY BODY
WITH THE FOLLOWING HEALTHY MEALS:**

_____ **FREE FLOW / REFLECTION** _____

✳ SACRED SPACE ✳

REFLECT, SET INTENTIONS, OR FREE-FLOW JOURNAL.

I HAVE THE STRENGTH TO GROW THROUGH MY WEAKNESSES

WEEK BEGINNING _____

I LOVE MYSELF BECAUSE:

1. _____

2. _____

3. _____

EMPOWERING AFFIRMATION:

THIS WEEK FOR SELF-CARE I WILL:

_____

_____

_____

_____

THIS WEEK I CHALLENGE MYSELF TO:

_____

_____

_____

THE HOBBY I WILL MAKE TIME FOR IS:

_____

_____

**I WILL NOURISH MY BODY
WITH THE FOLLOWING HEALTHY MEALS:**

_____ **FREE FLOW / REFLECTION** _____

WEEK BEGINNING _____

I LOVE MYSELF BECAUSE:

1.
_____

2.
_____

3.
_____

EMPOWERING AFFIRMATION:

THIS WEEK FOR SELF-CARE I WILL:

_____

_____

_____

_____

THIS WEEK I CHALLENGE MYSELF TO:

_____

_____

_____

THE HOBBY I WILL MAKE TIME FOR IS:

_____

_____

I WILL NOURISH MY BODY
WITH THE FOLLOWING HEALTHY MEALS:

_____ **FREE FLOW / REFLECTION** _____

✳ SACRED SPACE ✳

REFLECT, SET INTENTIONS, OR FREE-FLOW JOURNAL.

I take * time to do the things * that make my SOUL HAPPY

WEEK BEGINNING _____

I LOVE MYSELF BECAUSE:

1. _____

2. _____

3. _____

EMPOWERING AFFIRMATION:

THIS WEEK FOR SELF-CARE I WILL:

_____

_____

_____

_____

THIS WEEK I CHALLENGE MYSELF TO:

_____

_____

_____

THE HOBBY I WILL MAKE TIME FOR IS:

_____

_____

I WILL NOURISH MY BODY
WITH THE FOLLOWING HEALTHY MEALS:

_____ **FREE FLOW / REFLECTION** _____

WEEK BEGINNING _____

I LOVE MYSELF BECAUSE:

1.
_____

2.
_____

3.
_____

EMPOWERING AFFIRMATION:

THIS WEEK FOR SELF-CARE I WILL:

_____

_____

_____

_____

THIS WEEK I CHALLENGE MYSELF TO:

_____

_____

_____

THE HOBBY I WILL MAKE TIME FOR IS:

_____

_____

I WILL NOURISH MY BODY
WITH THE FOLLOWING HEALTHY MEALS:

_____ FREE FLOW / REFLECTION _____

✳ SACRED SPACE ✳

REFLECT, SET INTENTIONS, OR FREE-FLOW JOURNAL.

I AM
LOVED

WEEK BEGINNING _____

I LOVE MYSELF BECAUSE:

1. _____

2. _____

3. _____

EMPOWERING AFFIRMATION:

```
+---------------------------------------------------+
|                                                   |
|                                                   |
|                                                   |
|                                                   |
+---------------------------------------------------+
```

THIS WEEK FOR SELF-CARE I WILL:

_____

_____

_____

_____

THIS WEEK I CHALLENGE MYSELF TO:

_____

_____

_____

THE HOBBY I WILL MAKE TIME FOR IS:

_____

_____

I WILL NOURISH MY BODY
WITH THE FOLLOWING HEALTHY MEALS:

_____ FREE FLOW / REFLECTION _____

WEEK BEGINNING _____

I LOVE MYSELF BECAUSE:

1. _____

2. _____

3. _____

EMPOWERING AFFIRMATION:

THIS WEEK FOR SELF-CARE I WILL:

_____

_____

_____

_____

THIS WEEK I CHALLENGE MYSELF TO:

_____

_____

_____

THE HOBBY I WILL MAKE TIME FOR IS:

_____

_____

I WILL NOURISH MY BODY
WITH THE FOLLOWING HEALTHY MEALS:

_____ FREE FLOW / REFLECTION _____

✳ SACRED SPACE ✳

REFLECT, SET INTENTIONS, OR FREE-FLOW JOURNAL.

I GIVE MYSELF THE LOVE AND SPACE I NEED TO HEAL

WEEK BEGINNING _____

I LOVE MYSELF BECAUSE:

1. _____

2. _____

3. _____

EMPOWERING AFFIRMATION:

```
┌─────────────────────────────────────────────┐
│                                               │
│                                               │
│                                               │
│                                               │
└─────────────────────────────────────────────┘
```

THIS WEEK FOR SELF-CARE I WILL:

_____

_____

_____

_____

THIS WEEK I CHALLENGE MYSELF TO:

_____

_____

_____

THE HOBBY I WILL MAKE TIME FOR IS:

_____

_____

**I WILL NOURISH MY BODY
WITH THE FOLLOWING HEALTHY MEALS:**

FREE FLOW / REFLECTION

WEEK BEGINNING _____

I LOVE MYSELF BECAUSE:

1. _____

2. _____

3. _____

EMPOWERING AFFIRMATION:

THIS WEEK FOR SELF-CARE I WILL:

_____

_____

_____

_____

THIS WEEK I CHALLENGE MYSELF TO:

_____

_____

_____

THE HOBBY I WILL MAKE TIME FOR IS:

_____

_____

I WILL NOURISH MY BODY
WITH THE FOLLOWING HEALTHY MEALS:

_____   **FREE FLOW / REFLECTION**   _____

✳ SACRED SPACE ✳

REFLECT, SET INTENTIONS, OR FREE-FLOW JOURNAL.

I am calm
I am centered
I am peaceful

WEEK BEGINNING _____

I LOVE MYSELF BECAUSE:

1. _____

2. _____

3. _____

EMPOWERING AFFIRMATION:

THIS WEEK FOR SELF-CARE I WILL:

_____

_____

_____

_____

THIS WEEK I CHALLENGE MYSELF TO:

_____

_____

_____

THE HOBBY I WILL MAKE TIME FOR IS:

_____

_____

I WILL NOURISH MY BODY
WITH THE FOLLOWING HEALTHY MEALS:

_____ FREE FLOW / REFLECTION _____

WEEK BEGINNING _____

I LOVE MYSELF BECAUSE:

1. _____

2. _____

3. _____

EMPOWERING AFFIRMATION:

THIS WEEK FOR SELF-CARE I WILL:

_____

_____

_____

_____

THIS WEEK I CHALLENGE MYSELF TO:

_____

_____

_____

THE HOBBY I WILL MAKE TIME FOR IS:

_____

_____

I WILL NOURISH MY BODY
WITH THE FOLLOWING HEALTHY MEALS:

_____ **FREE FLOW / REFLECTION** _____

✳ SACRED SPACE ✳

REFLECT, SET INTENTIONS, OR FREE-FLOW JOURNAL.

I AM AMAZING JUST AS I AM

✳ ABOUT THE AUTHOR ✳

Photograph of the author by Joanne Crawford

Kelsey Layne is a designer and self-confessed journal/stationery lover. As the founder of Note and Shine, she is bringing her vision of beautifully designed, user-friendly journals and paper products into the world, including *The Manifestation Journal* and *The Evening Rituals Journal*. She lives in York, England.

An imprint of Penguin Random House LLC
penguinrandomhouse.com

Most TarcherPerigee books are available at special quantity discounts for bulk
purchase for sales promotions, premiums, fund-raising, and educational needs.
Special books or book excerpts also can be created to fit specific needs. For
details, write SpecialMarkets@penguinrandomhouse.com.

Trade paperback ISBN: 9780593543603

Printed in the United States of America
1st Printing

Book design by Kelsey Layne